THE ROSARY

Moreno Dal Bello

THE ROSARY

"Everyone knows how thoroughly Romanist is the use of the Rosary; and how the devotees of Rome mechanically tell their prayers upon their beads. The Rosary, however, is no invention of the papacy. It is of the highest antiquity, and almost universally found among Pagan nations."
Alexander Hislop

WHAT IS THE ROSARY?

The Rosary is at once a series of prayers and also a string of 55 beads used to count these prayers as they are recited (the larger version of the Rosary has 165 beads).

In its full version, the Rosary consists of 15 Paternosters (the Lord's Prayer), which are addressed to God the Father; 15 Glorias and an extraordinary **150** Hail Marys! which are, of course, addressed to Mary, the mother of Jesus. The Prayer to Mary is repeated 10 times to every one recital of the Lord's Prayer. **Ralph Woodrow**, author of the book *Babylon Mystery Religion: Ancient and Modern*, poses the question which every Roman Catholic needs to ask himself, and that is: *"...is a prayer composed by men and directed to Mary ten times as important or effective as the prayer taught by Jesus and directed to God?"*[1]

One would think that a prayer of such importance according to Roman Catholic teaching, would have been around since the inception of Christianity. This, however, is not the case. Even *The Catholic Encyclopedia* readily admits to the fact that: *"There is little or no trace of the 'Hail Mary' as an accepted devotional formula before about 1050 A.D."*[2]

The more common Rosary beads, usually found in white, gold or black, consist of a string or chain of beads divided into 5 sections, each made up of one large bead and 10 smaller ones. The larger Rosary has 15 sections.

The ends of the Rosary chain are joined by a medal decorated with an embossed image of Mary. From this medal hangs a short chain of beads, at the end of which is attached a crucifix.

As the shorter Rosary, which contains only 5 sections, is the more common of the two, it is prayed through 3 times, thus completing the full Rosary. The more devout Roman Catholics recite the Rosary daily.

Loraine Boettner, author of the classic book *Roman Catholicism*, explains the process: *"Holding the large bead of each section in turn, one says the Our Father, and, holding the small beads, the Hail Mary for each separate bead. Between each section the Gloria is said..."*[3]

THE ORIGIN AND HISTORY OF THE ROSARY

'Rosary' is an ancient word meaning *a garland* (of roses or leaves etc.). Legend has it that the beads were originally made of Rosewood. Today, they may be made of glass or even stone. The Rosary

was first implemented by the Roman Catholic Church in the year 1090 A.D., over 1,000 years *after* the death and resurrection of the Lord Jesus Christ.

The Roman Catholic Church herself has acknowledged that the Rosary did not come into general use until the 13th century, and the practice was not officially sanctioned by the Roman Church until after the Protestant Reformation in the 16th century.

The exact time and place in regard to the origin of the rosary, or prayer beads, is difficult to trace. However, we do know that Buddhists and Muslims had been using a device for counting prayers similar to the rosary centuries before the Rosary was introduced to Roman Catholics.

According to unchallengeable historical fact, the rosary is a device which originated in Paganism and is commonly found throughout the many and varied religions of the world. Clearly, the concept of prayer beads or prayer counters had been in use for centuries, long before the Roman Catholic Church decided to continue this popular pagan tradition, furnishing it with a Christian veneer.

Roman Catholics cannot argue this point, for their own Church approved *Catholic Encyclopedia* states: *"In almost all countries, then, we meet with something in the nature of prayer counters or rosary-beads."*[4] The same article cites a number of examples including a sculpture of ancient Nineveh, of two winged females praying before a sacred tree, each holding a rosary!

The Roman Catholic Encyclopedia also makes mention of a bead-string made up of 33, 66 or 99 beads which has for centuries been used by Muslims for counting the names of Allah, the Muslim god. Marco Polo, way back in the 13th century, was startled to find the king of Malabar using a rosary made of precious stones to count his prayers. Equally amazed were founding members of the Jesuits, St. Francis Xavier and his companions when, in their travels, they discovered that the Buddhists of Japan were also familiar with the rosary.

Ralph Woodrow reports that, *"Among the Phoenicians a circle of beads resembling a rosary was used in the worship of Astarte, the mother goddess, about 800 B.C.! This rosary may also be found on some early Phoenician coins. The Brahmans* (worshippers of one of the many Indian gods) *have from early times used rosaries made up of tens of hundreds of beads. The worshippers of Vishnu* (another false Indian god) *give their children rosaries of 108 beads. A similar rosary is used by millions of Buddhists in India and Tibet. The worshipper of Siva* (yet another Indian god) *uses a rosary upon which he repeats, if possible, all the 1,008 names of his god."*[5]

Followers of the Sikh religion, which developed in the 15th century in North India as a synthesis of Islam and Buddhism, also employ the use of prayer beads in their worship time. One painting depicts a raja worshipping the Hindu god,

Rama, whilst holding a rosary. The rosary also features prominently in a 19th century painting from India of a Hindu ascetic.

The rosary was also part of the religious life of the ancient Mexicans. It was considered a sacred religious instrument. Reference is made frequently in sacred Hindu books of the rosary. Also, the Tartar religion of the Lamas in China use a rosary of 108 beads as part of their ceremonial dress.

Alexander Hislop, author of the highly recommended book *The Two Babylons*, an exhaustive investigation into the origins of Roman Catholic teaching and practices, makes the following significant observation that the Rosary requires, *"...that a certain number of prayers must be regularly gone over; it overlooks the great demand which God makes for the heart, and leads those who use them to believe that form and routine are everything, and that 'they must be heard for their much speaking.'"*[6]

WHAT DOES THE ROMAN CATHOLIC BIBLE SAY?

Nowhere in the Roman Catholic Bible is any mention made of prayer beads. In fact, no mention of any kind of 'instrument' or 'prayer aid' is made. These things belong to the realm of paganism and have nothing to do with the true Christian Faith.

Neither does the Word of God in any way support or condone such a means of prayer as the

Rosary. In fact, Matthew 6:7 is where we find Jesus actually condemning the act of repetitious prayer. Jesus Christ says: **"In praying, do not babble like the pagans, who think they will be heard because of their many words."** In the original Greek text, the word used for *babble* is *battaloge* meaning (vain) *repetitions*. In other words, Jesus warns His people that they should not pray like the pagans who use vain repetitions, meaning *"...do not be saying idle things i.e., meaningless and mechanically repeated phrases!"*[7]

Jesus was here explaining to His followers that they were not to be as the pagans, who think that God will hear them because of their many words (cf. Ecclesiastes 5:1,2). With utter disregard to the command of the Lord Jesus, Roman Catholic priests instruct and encourage their parishioners to pray the prayers of the Rosary repetitiously on a daily basis. **Alexander Hislop** states that *"...in giving penances after confession they* (the priests) *often assign a certain number of Hail Marys to be said.* (It is taught that) *the more such prayers are said the more merit is stored up in heaven."*[8]

Although the Lord Jesus Christ did not formally fix the length that His follower's prayers should be, according to His own words that we have just seen in Matthew 6:7, Jesus **did** command that His people **should not repeat the same prayer over and over** as though God did not hear us, or as if He would be moved merely by our much speaking. It is interesting to note that after instructing His disciples not to pray repetitiously, Jesus taught the Apostles how to pray by introducing them to the Lord's Prayer (Matthew 6:7-13). In literal defiance, the Roman Catholic Church blatantly ignores this teaching of Jesus Christ and instead instructs her followers to pray even this prayer repetitiously!

As **Woodrow** has said, *"If this prayer* (the Lord's Prayer), *was not to be repeated over and over, how much less a little mandate prayer to Mary!"*[9]

It is stated in John 4:23 that the true worshippers of God would **"...worship the Father in spirit and truth."** *"Spiritual worship is that where the heart is offered to God, and where we do not depend on external forms for acceptance."*[10] Worshipping the Father *in truth* is worshipping Him directly through the true and only Way, Jesus Christ (see John 14:6).

Many people have been deceived into believing that all is right with their souls as long as they perform a substantial amount of 'religious duties', including such 'duties' as praying the Rosary. God is not so much interested in our words as He is with our hearts. Merely reciting the same words over and over to Him is not, and has never been, a Christian practice and is wholly condemned in the Bible.

The great danger in repetitious praying is that it can easily become a mere speaking to God, words from the mouth rather than words from the heart. The true believer need not say much in prayer, for Jesus goes on to say in Matthew 6:8,

"*Do not be like them* (the heathen). ***Your Father knows what you need before you ask Him.***" Ecclesiastes 5:1 says in part: "***...God is in heaven and you are on earth; therefore let your words be few.***"

Even if the Rosary were a biblically legitimate form of prayer, the same words need not be prayed over and over. Jesus clearly speaks against this in Matthew 6, condemning it as a pagan practice.

Loraine Boettner wisely states: *"The Bible teaches that the true believer should pray to God reverently, humbly, and with a believing and thankful heart, thinking of what he is doing and of the great King to whom he is praying. It is a distinguishing mark of Roman Catholicism, and also a matter of primary importance between Romanism and Protestantism, that a Roman Catholic 'says' or 'recites' his prayers, while for the most part the Protestant speaks extemporaneously, with his own words, thinking out his praise, petitions, requests, and thanks as he prays. <u>For a spiritually minded person the mechanical use of beads destroys the true spirit of prayer.</u>"*[11]

PRAYERS TO MARY?

I felt it important at this point to pay particular attention to the fact that in the numerous prayers which make up the Rosary, the number of prayers that are directed to **Mary** far outweigh those addressed to God the Father. The ratio is 10 to 1!

Even more remarkable is the fact that there are **NO prayers at all in the Rosary addressed to the Lord Jesus Christ or even prayed in His name!**

The Bible, God's Holy and infallible Word, is quite clear in its instructions concerning prayer. Even in the Roman Catholic Bible the Lord Jesus is quoted as saying: **"...I say to you, whatever you ask <u>the Father</u> in My name He will give you. Until now you have not asked anything in My name; ask and you will receive, so that your joy may be complete"** (John 16:23b,24). And in John 14:14 Jesus says, **"If you ask anything of Me in My Name, I will do it."** We see then, from the very words of Jesus Christ, the only instructions that Jesus gives concerning whom prayer is to be directed towards, is either the Father in Jesus' name or to Jesus Himself in His own name. It is vital for the Roman Catholic to realise that **THERE ARE NO INSTRUCTIONS IN THE ENTIRE ROMAN CATHOLIC BIBLE TO PRAY TO ANY OTHER, NOT EVEN TO MARY!!**

THE PAGAN WAY IS NOT THE CHRISTIAN WAY

We believe we have provided clear and indisputable evidence that the use of the Rosary has no basis in Holy Scripture and that it is not even a Roman Catholic invention, but is in fact of pagan origin. Moreover, we have seen that the Roman Catholic Church freely admits to this in *The Catholic Encyclopedia*. Though many practices and traditions in the Church of Rome originate from paganism, a fact which Roman Catholic scholars readily admit to, the attitude is that it is perfectly logical and valid to take the old pagan rites and practices of the heathen and, with them, worship the true God.

In other words, the argument put forth by the Roman Catholic Church is that, if pagans worship their false gods by burning candles or using prayer beads, why then can't we worship the true God in the same way. **Woodrow** illustrates further, *'If some pagan tribe observed 40 days in honor of a pagan god, why should we not do the same, only in honor of Christ? Though pagans worshipped the sun towards the east, could we not have sunrise services to honor the resurrection of Christ, even though this was not the true time of day He arose. In other words, why not adopt all kinds of popular customs, only instead of using them to honor pagan gods, as the heathen did, use them to honor Christ?"*[12]

Pagans also worshipped and prayed to a mother-goddess. Roman Catholicism has copied the popular practice of mother worship, replacing pagan goddesses such as the Egyptian Isis, or Astarte and Diana, with a Christian identity, Mary.

The pagans also had various gods and goddesses who were individually associated with specific days, occupations and events in life. This pagan tradition has also been faithfully continued by the Roman Catholic Church, the 'gods', so-called, being replaced with 'saints'. Throughout history heathen religions have also bowed down to and worshipped statues and idols of pagan deities. The Roman Catholic Church does exactly the same, though calling them by different names. The well known statue of 'St. Peter' in Rome was formerly recognized as a statue of the Roman god Jupiter. **Many of the old pagan gods of time past are alive and well today, hidden in Roman Catholic saints!**

As was mentioned earlier, the Roman Catholic Church does not deny that many of its most popular practices originated in pagan religions. *The Catholic Encyclopedia* states the following: *"We need not shrink from admitting that candles, incense and lustral* ('holy') *water, were commonly employed in pagan worship and in the rites paid to the dead. But the* (Roman Catholic) *Church from a very early period took them into her service, just as she adapted many other things...like music, lights, perfumes, ablutions, floral decorations, canopies, fans, screens, bells, vestments, etc., which were not identified with any idolatrous cult in particular; THEY WERE COMMON TO ALMOST ALL CULTS!"*[13]

The same publication also freely admits that, *"Water, oil, lights, incense, singing, procession, prostration, decoration of altars, vestments or priests, are naturally at the service of universal religious instinct..."*[14] Now to the natural man, this does sound logical. But to the spirit-filled born again believer, it is recognized as an evil concept. Our next chapter will explain.

HOW NOT TO WORSHIP GOD

The whole concept of worshipping the One True God in the same manner as pagans worship their false gods, is utterly detestable in the sight of God. **It is an unacceptable form of worship.** The true God **must** be worshipped according to the directives **He** has given in His Holy Word, the Bible, and not in accordance with how a man may think or feel at the time, no matter how sincere he is. **Sincerity never justifies the means, nor does it make up for a belief in a false gospel and therefore a false god.** An ignorance founded on sincerity is no grounds for pardon from God but only further condemns the believer of false teachings and practitioner of ungodly pagan traditions.

We learn this from God's very own Words, recorded for us in Deuteronomy 12:30,31: *"...**Do not inquire regarding their gods, 'How did these nations worship their gods? I too, would do the same.' YOU SHALL NOT THUS WORSHIP THE LORD, YOUR GOD, because they offered to their gods every abomination that the Lord detests...**"* The abominations here spoken of that the Lord detests are the very methods and religious inventions which come from the mind of man and are considered as proper and right worship of God. **You CANNOT come to God on your own terms or based on ungodly traditions, but only in accordance with what God has said.**

And in Deuteronomy 13:1, God says: **"Every command that I enjoin on you, you shall be careful to observe, NEITHER ADDING TO IT NOR SUBTRACTING FROM IT."** (cf. Deuteronomy 13:18; Proverbs 30:6; Revelation 22:18,19). THERE IS NO PLACE FOR THE INVENTIONS OF MAN IN THE WORSHIP OF GOD. **Without true saving Faith one cannot please God** (see Hebrews 11:6).

We see an example of this kind of prohibited worship exhibited by Israel in the Old Testament. In Exodus 32 we are told of their fashioning a golden calf. In verse 5 we see Aaron proclaiming, **"...tomorrow is a feast of the Lord (Jehovah)."** The Jews did not presume that the image they had made was in itself a god, but they had made it to represent the true God, whom they thought they could worship through the image of the golden calf. God has expressly forbidden this form of worship. The second commandment of God says: **"You shall not carve idols for yourselves in the shape of anything in the sky above or in the earth below or in the waters beneath the earth; YOU SHALL NOT BOW DOWN BEFORE THEM OR WORSHIP THEM..."** (Exodus 20:4,5a). Significantly, while THIS COMMANDMENT IS QUOTED FROM THE ROMAN CATHOLIC BIBLE, IT IS STRANGELY OMITTED IN MOST CATHOLIC CATECHISM'S LISTS OF THE TEN COMMANDMENTS and the majority of Roman Catholic approved books which carry the Imprimatur!

Further examples of Israel displeasing God by following the traditions of heathen nations and incorporating their manner of worship, may be found in 2 Kings 17:15, where we are told that Israel had *"...followed the surrounding nations WHOM THE LORD HAD COMMANDED THEM NOT TO IMITATE."* In Jeremiah 10:2 we see God's warning to His people, *"Thus saith the Lord, LEARN NOT THE CUSTOMS OF THE NATIONS..."* **In other words it is God's command that HIS people have nothing whatsoever to do with the religious teachings, traditions, customs and practices of any who are not His people** (see Romans 16:17; 2 John 10,11).

In all this we see clearly that one way the Christian is most definitely NOT to worship the true God is in the same manner that the pagans, the heathen nations, worship their false gods. This immediately rules out the use of the Rosary, as well as many other paganistic Roman Catholic practices such as candle burning, the mother-goddess worship of Mary and other heathen inventions.

These practices, however much they may be accompanied by sincerity to worship and please the true God, can never do so. God Himself has said in reation to the way pagans worship their false gods: *"YOU SHALL NOT THUS WORSHIP THE LORD YOUR GOD"* (Deuteronomy 12:31).

COME OUT FROM HER....

The purpose of this booklet has not been to judge or condemn you, the Roman Catholic, but has been designed to educate you, to inform you of facts and proper biblical teaching which the Roman Catholic Church has not given you. It has been written in order to provide you with historical facts about the origins of many of your Church's teachings and traditions. **You have read for yourself what the Roman Catholic Church admits to and what your own Roman Catholic Bible says, and doesn't say—what it teaches and simply does not support.** Ultimately, this booklet is a plea for you to come out of the Roman Catholic Church, away from all its man-made doctrines and pagan practices, away from its false gospel. **God must be worshipped HIS way, for no other way is acceptable unto Him.** There is no other way to worship the true God—**and therefore be a saved, justified and true follower of God**—other than the way He has prescribed in His Holy Word. **There is no Gospel that must be believed, by which a man is saved, other than the one that reveals the Righteousness of Christ.**

We have presented the truth to you. **Verifiable truth.** We have quoted from many sources approved by your own Church including a Church approved Bible. But do not believe things simply because you saw them written in a booklet. The Bible commends those who properly investigate what is presented to them as truth and we encourage you to do so. In Acts 17:11 the apostle Paul and Silas preached to the people at Berea. The Roman Catholic Bible says that **"These...were more fair-minded than those in Thessalonica, for they received the word with all willingness and EXAMINED THE SCRIPTURES DAILY TO DETERMINE WHETHER THESE THINGS WERE SO."** The Scriptures were their sole authority. They did not refer to the writings of mere men, seeking out their opinions, but went immediately to the Holy Word of God **knowing** that His Word alone could be trusted, and was the sure test for all teachings being presented as God's own decrees (see 2 Peter 1:19). Paul and Silas were not offended by their examining and putting to the test what they were saying, they did not say *'How dare you examine what we have said to you; don't you know who we are?'* **Every Christian, indeed every person, is to examine by the Holy Scriptures all that is presented to him as God's teaching, and if it does not match with the Scriptures, you can be sure it did not come from God and is to be rejected out of hand.** Writing to true believers, John said, **"Beloved, DO NOT TRUST every spirit BUT TEST the spirits to see whether they belong to God, because many false prophets have gone out into the world"** (1 John 4:1).

The subtle deceptiveness of the Roman Catholic Church is that she teaches some truths of Scripture but always adds to them, something which the Scriptures roundly condemn: **"Add**

NOTHING to HIS Words, lest He reprove you, and you be exposed as a deceiver" (Proverbs 30:6). In speaking against such deception the Lord Jesus warned His disciples to **"...Look out, and beware of the leaven of the Pharisees and Sadducees"** (Matthew 16:6 cf. Galatians 5:9). Later, the disciples **"...understood that He was not telling them to beware of the leaven of bread, but of THE TEACHING of the Pharisees and Sadducees"** (Matthew 16:12). The Pharisees and Sadducees were the religious leaders in Jesus' day. The apostle Paul warned: **"...watch out for those who create dissensions and obstacles, in opposition to the teaching that you learned; avoid them. For such people do not serve our Lord Christ but their own appetites, and by fair and flattering speech they deceive the hearts of the innocent"** (Romans 16:17,18). EXAMINE EVERYTHING! TEST EVERYTHING BY THE WORD OF GOD! **For we are dealing with eternal issues here. We are dealing with heaven and hell, and what a person believes determines their eternal destiny, for the doctrine you hold to is the surest evidence of whether or not it is the true God Who has revealed Himself to you or whether it is a false god whom you have embraced.**

Some examples of such deceptiveness are as follows: the Roman Catholic Church teaches her followers to pray the Lord's prayer, but they are encouraged to do so whilst holding the Rosary which is a pagan invention and has nothing to do with true Christianity. Yes, Rome agrees that God alone forgives sin, but they add that this power to forgive has been given to her priests and one must go *to them* to receive it and not directly to God the Father through Jesus His Son, as the Scriptures prescribe. Yes, Roman Catholicism teaches that the Bible is the Word of God but it considers tradition to be *equal* to God's precious Holy Word and insists that she is the only true interpreter of Scripture! **In other words, what ROME says God's Word is saying is what is to be obeyed, rather than what the Scripture's interpretation of Itself is saying! Compare Scripture with Scripture, not Scripture with a man's interpretation.** All along, Roman Catholicism adds to God's Word and in other instances withholds certain parts of it, such as the second Commandment, from its publications. It is true that Roman Catholicism teaches 'the death, burial and resurrection' of Jesus Christ but it is vitally important to note that while she may correctly teach some aspects of these things— things which are aligned with historical fact—the Roman Catholic Church **does not** teach the death, burial and resurrection of Jesus Christ ***"...in accordance with the Scriptures..."*** (1 Corinthians 15:3,4).

It is no accident that so much pagan tradition is found today in Roman Catholicism. It has been carefully managed and seen to, that old pagan/occultic rites and traditions, which the Bible calls demonic, are continued to be adhered to and promoted as vigilantly as they were by the early pagans, but now with a Christian veneer thus setting up the Roman Catholic Church as the unmistakably identifiable anti-christian system referred to as 'Babylon' in the Bible. Roman Catholicism stands today not only against Christ, for it does not teach His Gospel, but Rome has also, in a most vulgar way, usurped Christ's position. The papacy claims that **it** is the vicar of Christ on earth, rather than the Holy Spirit as the Word of God says.

That which immediately reveals a religious organization's ungodly foundation may be seen in the gospel it teaches. What a person, or organization such as the Roman Catholic Church, says about **Who Jesus Christ is, what He has done and for whom He has done it**—in other words His Person and His Work—will reveal whether or not that person or organization is of God (see 2 John 9). After having preached to them the True and only Gospel of salvation which reveals the true God and true Christ, Paul the apostle warned the believers in Galatia that ***"...even if we or an angel from heaven should preach to you a gospel OTHER THAN the one that we preached to you, let that one be accursed"*** (Galatians 1:8).

There are many who by nature are religious; many who are extremely zealous for what they believe to be the things of God, yet Scripture reminds us that by nature ***"There is no one just, not one, there is no one who understands, there is no one who seeks God"*** (Romans 3:10,11). Saving, God-given faith in the true and only Gospel of God shows that it is the true God Who has revealed Himself. **Belief in any gospel other than that one and only Gospel of God reveals that it is not the true God Who has revealed Himself but rather a false god who cannot save.**

We implore you to come out of the Roman Catholic Church. A Church which is headed, not by the Lord Jesus Christ, for it does not promote His Gospel, but by a man who calls himself the 'Pope', and who allows himself to be addressed as 'Holy Father', a title which God **ALONE** is worthy. God ALONE is Father, and God ALONE is Holy. The Lord Jesus only ever referred to God as 'Father', and in Revelation 15:4 Jesus, praying to the Father said: *"...You ALONE are Holy..."* How dare ANY man take upon himself a title of which ONLY God is worthy! Not incidentally, the Lord Jesus Christ also said to His followers not to call any man on earth father, that is in a spiritual sense, for One was their Father and He resides in heaven: **"Call no one on earth your father; you have but one Father in heaven"** (Matthew 23:9). Roman Catholicism responds to these words of the Lord Jesus by calling *every one of its priests 'father',* and demanding that everyone else, Roman Catholic or not, do likewise, despite admitting in their footnotes to Matthew 23:9 that *"...Jesus forbids not only the titles (rabbi, father and master) but the spirit of superiority and pride that is shown by their acceptance."*

Pope Leo XIII once blasphemously declared: *"The Pope holds upon this earth the place of God Almighty..."* **Robert Bellermine**, famous Jesuit Cardinal of the 16th century and also a saint of the Roman Catholic Church, had this to say: *"All the names which in the Scriptures are applied to Christ by virtue of which it is established that He is over the Church, all the same names are applied to the Pope."* The *Catholique Nationale* of Paris, in its July 13, 1895 issue, contained the following claim made by the then archbishop of Venice, later to become Pope Pius X. He said, *"The Pope is not only the representative of Jesus Christ, but he is Jesus Christ Himself hidden under the veil of the flesh..."* Dear Roman Catholic, **the Pope is NOT Jesus Christ! JESUS CHRIST IS GOD!! ONLY through the Lord Jesus Christ is there salvation, not through the Pope and his 'church' of Rome.**

"*History is replete with sayings that mocked Romanism's false claim to celibacy: 'The holiest hermit has his whore'*" and "'*Rome has more prostitutes than any other city because she has the most celibates*'" are examples. Pope Pius II called Rome '*The only city run by bastards, the sons and grandsons of popes and cardinals'*.

"Even Roman Catholic historians admit that among the popes were some of the most degenerate and unconscionable ogres in all history. More than one pope was slain by a husband who found him in bed with his wife. To call such a man 'His holiness vicar of Christ' makes a mockery of holiness and Christ. Yet the name of each of these mass murderers, fornicators, robbers, warmongers—some guilty of the massacre of thousands—is emblazoned in honor on the Church's official list of Peter's alleged successors, the popes" ('The Berean Call', July '94, p.2).

"Will you believe the words of the Roman Catholic Church or will you believe the words of the Roman Catholic Bible? It is for you to decide. Remember, there are only two religions in the entire world, man's and God's. If it is not the truth of God that you are believing, then you have embraced the lies of the Devil." **You have embraced a false gospel wherein is no salvation.** "Man's religion is by works—his own efforts, his fastings and prayers, his obedience to the Church. That, in effect, makes him his own saviour. God's is by faith in the finished work of Jesus Christ. Jesus paid it all... The Roman Catholic Bible states clearly: "...**we have been JUSTIFIED BY FAITH, we have peace with God through our Lord Jesus Christ**...Romans 5:1." The Roman Catholic Bible makes it perfectly clear that man cannot save himself and that Christ is his only hope; his only Saviour."[15]

"Salvation is not dependent on a human priest, Mary, Baptism, the saints, the sacraments, the Mass, confession, good works, membership in the Roman Catholic Church or the Pope."

Salvation is not gained by our loyalty or service to a person—**be they our parents or grandparents and their religious traditions which they have passed down to us**—or to an institution such as the Roman Catholic Church, but rather by our **acceptance of the truth**!! *"Jesus said:* **"...I am the Way and the Truth and the Life. No one comes to the Father EXCEPT THROUGH ME"** *(John 14:6)* and **"I am the Gate. Whoever enters through Me will be saved..."** (John 10:9). Acts 4:12 says: **'There is NO salvation through ANYONE else, nor is there ANY other name under heaven given to the human race by which we are to be saved.'**

It matters not how religious a person is or how sincere he might be in his religious pursuits, if a man has not the Gospel of God, if he does not **"...remain in the teaching of the Christ** (he) **does not have God..."** (2 John 9). **"That all who have not believed the truth but have approved wrongdoing may be condemned"** (2 Thessalonians 2:12). Scripture also speaks of the vengeance that will be had upon the enemies of God **"...at the revelation of the Lord Jesus from heaven with His mighty angels, in blazing fire, inflicting punishment on those who do not acknowledge God and on those WHO DO NOT OBEY THE GOSPEL of our Lord Jesus. These will pay the penalty of eternal ruin, separated from the presence of the Lord and from the glory of His power"** (2 Thessalonians 1:7-9).

Only through the Gospel of Christ wherein is revealed the Righteousness of Christ, without which no man can be saved, is there true salvation: **"For I am not ashamed of the Gospel. IT IS THE POWER OF GOD for the salvation of everyone who believes: for the**

Jew first, and then Greek. For in it is revealed the Righteousness of God from faith to faith; as it is written, the one who is righteous by faith will live" (Romans 1:16,17). Central to the Gospel message is the Person and Work of Jesus Christ and, according to the Scriptures, if one is wrong about Christ, if one has embraced erroneous doctrine concerning Christ the Person and His Work, one is not merely in need of correction yet nevertheless saved, one has in fact fallen for another jesus who is identified by false doctrine, and thus remains in a lost state. **Only in the True Jesus is their salvation. Belief, however sincere, in a false jesus CANNOT SAVE!** You see, not only does the apostle Paul state that the Gospel is the power of God but he also defines this statement in 1 Corinthians 1:18: ***"THE MESSAGE OF THE CROSS is foolishness to those who are perishing, but to us who are being saved IT*** (THE CROSS) ***IS THE POWER OF GOD."***

Belief in false doctrines concerning Christ constitutes a belief in *another* gospel, one which does not represent the true Christ but a false savior (see 2 Corinthians 11:3,4). The Holy Spirit is the Spirit of Truth (John 14:17; 15:26; 16:13) and never presents a man with, nor leads him to believe, a false gospel: ***"But when He comes, the Spirit of Truth, He will guide you to all truth..."*** (John 16:13). Jesus prayed, ***"Consecrate them in the Truth. Your Word is Truth"*** (John 17:17). The true believer is consecrated, or sanctified, through the truth which is the Word of God and not through the lies of men. Speaking to saved men, the apostle Paul stated: **"...God chose you as the firstfruits for salvation through sanctification BY THE SPIRIT <u>AND</u> BELIEF IN TRUTH"** (2 Thessalonians 2:13). There is no true sanctification if one's faith is not in the Truth of God.

Only by belief in Christ's Gospel, which says that man is dead in sin, without God and without hope of salvation by anything he is or does in an effort to please God and gain His favor, is a man saved: **"Therefore, remember that at one time you...were at that time without Christ...without hope and without God in the world"** (Ephesians 2:11-13). **"You were dead in your transgressions and sins"** (Ephesians 2:1). **"All have sinned and are deprived of the glory of God"** (Romans 3:23).

Only by belief in Christ's Gospel, which says that a man is saved not by works, not by anything he has done, is doing or will do, but solely by the grace and mercy of God, is a man saved: **"...a person is not justified by works of the law but through faith in Jesus Christ, even we have believed in Christ Jesus that we may be justified by faith in Christ and not by works of the law, because by works of the law no one will be justified"** (Galatians 1:16). The cry of the truly justified sinner is that he is **"...justified freely by His grace through the redemption in Christ Jesus, Whom God set**

forth as an expiation, through faith, by His blood..." (Romans 3:24,25).

Only by belief in Christ's Gospel, which says a man is not saved based on anything he has done but solely by the grace of God through the election of grace, is a man saved: **"...God chose you as the firstfruits for salvation through sanctification by the Spirit and belief in truth"** (2 Thessalonians 2:13). **"As He chose us in Him, before the foundation of the world, to be holy and without blemish before Him"** (Ephesians 1:4); **"He saved us and called us to a holy life, NOT ACCORDING TO OUR WORKS, but according to His own design and the grace bestowed on us in Christ Jesus before time began"** (2 Timothy 1:9). No saved person ever came to God first (see 1 John 4:19). In every case God came to the person first and gave them the gift of salvation, not because they had in any way earned this gift, but freely and only by the will of God and the grace of God. Scripture says that by nature **"...there is no one who seeks God"** (Romans 3:11). **"But when one does not work, yet believes in the One Who justifies the ungodly, his faith is credited as righteousness. So also David declares the blessedness of the person to whom God credits righteousness apart from works"** (Romans 4:5,6).

Only by belief in Christ's Gospel, which says that Christ died exclusively for His people, those whom God had given Him (see John 17:2), and has provided them with an atonement for their sin, having their sins imputed, or charged, to Him and imputing unto them His perfect righteousness, is a man saved. Jesus said: **"I am the good shepherd. A good shepherd lays down His life for the sheep....I will lay down My life for the sheep"** (John 10:11,15). Writing to true believers Paul said, **"For our sake He made Him to be sin** (for us) **who did not know sin, so that we might become the righteousness of God in Him"** (2 Corinthians 5:21).

Only by belief in Christ's Gospel, which says that all His people shall come to Him, hear and believe His Gospel, is there true salvation. None whom the Lord has given unto Him shall perish, none shall be plucked from His Hand, but all for whom He died shall be saved: **"My sheep hear My voice; I know them, and they follow Me. I give them eternal life, and they shall never perish. No one can take them out of My hand"** (John 10:27,28). **"Everything that the Father gives Me WILL come to Me..."** (John 6:37).

Only by belief in Christ's Gospel, which states that none for whom He died shall ever perish, but all who have had their sins charged to Him shall be given eternal life, is a man saved. Salvation has not only been *obtained* for God's chosen, but it is eternally *maintained* by the Will of God and all that Christ has done: **"...Give glory to Your Son, so that Your Son may glorify You, just as You gave Him authority over all people, so that He may give eternal life to all**

You gave Him" (John 17:1,2). Christ has not only obtained salvation for His people, by paying the penalty for their sin and imputing to them His righteousness, He also maintains their salvation by His eternal and completed work upon the cross. Thus ALL the glory for salvation belongs to God and none of it is shared with any man based on his works. **Only THIS Gospel gives ALL the glory to God for salvation and wherein there is no room for man to boast in anything he is or has done.**

Only by belief in Christ's Gospel, which states that no man is, or can be saved by his own righteousness, by his own efforts at obedience to God's Law, but only by the perfect Righteousness of Jesus Christ which is freely imputed based on His grace and mercy ALONE to all those for whom He died, is a man saved. The apostle Paul wanted to ***"...be found in Him, not having any righteousness of my own based on the law but that which comes through faith in Christ, the righteousness from God, depending on faith..."*** (Philippians 3:9). Paul considered all that he was and did in the realm of religion as rubbish, **and therefore himself as a lost person,** before knowing Christ and His Gospel: ***"...because of the supreme good of knowing Christ Jesus my Lord. For His sake I have accepted the loss of all things and I consider them so much rubbish..."*** (Philippians 3:8).

Only those who have heard the Word of Truth, God's Mighty Gospel, can be said to truly hope in the true Christ: ***"In Him you also, who*** *have heard the word of truth, **THE GOSPEL OF YOUR SALVATION,** and have believed in Him, were sealed with the promised Holy Spirit"* (Ephesians 1:13).

Look then to the only true Jesus Who is the Author and Finisher of the Faith which God gives and which only believes in the true Gospel.

ANY AND ALL FAITH IN ANOTHER JESUS WILL NOT SAVE.

ANY AND ALL FAITH IN ANOTHER GOSPEL WILL NOT SAVE.

"Whoever believes (THE Gospel) *and is baptized will be saved; whoever does not believe will be condemned"* (Mark 16:16).

The true born again believer knows that *"...by grace you have been saved through faith, and this is not from you; it is the gift of God; it is not from works, so no one may boast"* (Ephesians 2:8,9).

May God bless each and every one of you with His Truth as revealed in His Gospel.

NOTES

[1] Babylon Mystery Religion: Ancient and Modern, R.E. Woodrow, p.22, 1966, Ralph Woodrow Evangelistic Association, Inc.

[2] The Catholic Encyclopedia, Vol.7, p.111, article: 'Hail Mary'.

[3] Roman Catholicism, L. Boettner, p.284-285, 1962, Presbyterian and Reformed Publishing Company.

[4] The Catholic Encyclopedia, Vol.13, p.185, article: 'Rosary'.

[5] Babylon Mystery Religion, op.cit., p.21-22.

[6] The Two Babylons, Rev. A. Hislop, 1916, p.188, S.W. Partridge & Co.

[7] Vine's Complete Expository Dictionary of Old & New Testament Words, W.E. Vine, M.F. Unger, W. White, Jr., 1985, p.525, Thomas Nelson Publishers.

[8] The Two Babylons, op.cit., p.285.

[9] Babylon Mystery Religion, op.cit., p.22.

[10] Barnes' Notes on the New Testament, A. Barnes, 1962, p.283, Kregel.

[11] Roman Catholicism, op.cit., p.285.

[12] Babylon Mystery Religion, op.cit., p.140.

[13] The Catholic Encyclopedia, Vol.3, p.246, article: 'Candles'.

[14] Ibid, Vol.11, p.90, article: 'Paganism'.

[15] The Catholic Bible Has The Answer, op.cit., p.16.

Please Contact:

morenodalbello@yahoo.com.au

Please Visit:

www.godsonlygospel.com

Made in the USA
Monee, IL
03 May 2026